Life As ...

Life As a Cowboy in the American West

Laura L. Sullivan

Cavendish Square

New York

Published in 2016 by Cavendish Square Publishing, LLC
243 5th Avenue, Suite 136, New York, NY 10016

Library of Congress Cataloging-in-Publication Data

Sullivan, Laura L.
Life as a cowboy in the American west / Laura L. Sullivan.
pages cm. — (Life as...)
Includes bibliographical references and index.
ISBN 978-1-5026-1086-7 (hardcover) ISBN 978-1-5026-1072-0 (paperback) ISBN 978-1-5026-1087-4 (ebook)
1. Cowboys—West (U.S.)—Juvenile literature. 2. Frontier and pioneer life—West (U.S.)—Juvenile literature. I. Title.
F596.S925 2016
978'.02—dc23

2015017914

Editorial Director: David McNamara
Editor: Kristen Susienka
Copy Editor: Nathan Heidelberger
Art Director: Jeffrey Talbot
Designer: Joseph Macri
Senior Production Manager: Jennifer Ryder-Talbot
Production Editor: Renni Johnson
Photo Research: J8 Media

The photographs in this book are used by permission and through the courtesy of: Transcendental Graphics/Archive Photos/Getty Images, cover; Marco Mayer/Shutterstock.com, cover and used throughout the book; Transcendental Graphics/Archive Photos/Getty Images, 5; Public Domain/File:Vaqueros.jpg/Wikimedia Commons, 6; Library of Congress/File:Grabill - The Cow Boy.jpg/Wikimedia Commons, 9; Ernst Haas/Getty Images, 10; Herbert Orth/The LIFE Picture Collection/Getty Images, 11; Design Pics/Carson Ganci/Getty Images, 14; Didecs/Shutterstock.com, 16; Library of Congress, 17; John Lund/The Image Bank/Getty Images, 18; Cultura Travel/Ben Pipe Photography/Getty Images, 20; George Lepp/The Image Bank/Getty Images, 21; Courtesy of the Witte Museum, San Antonio, TX, 22; Kriss Russell/Thinkstock/iStock, 23; File:Branded.jpg/Wikimedia Commons, 24; Benjamin O'Neal/iStock/Thinkstock, 25; dgphotography/Thinkstock, 27.

Printed in the United States of America

Contents

Introduction

The cowboy—someone who herds cows while on horseback—is a symbol of the **American West**. He represents the freedom of a vast frontier and the determination of the American spirit. Being a cowboy was an important job in the nineteenth century. It was also a hard and dangerous job. Cowboys had to move huge herds of cattle, or cows, hundreds of miles from the ranch to the market or railway for sale. They faced deadly **stampedes** and ruthless cattle thieves. From the Mexican *vaqueros* to the rodeo stars of today, cowboys have been a central part of life out West.

The cowboy is an icon of the American West.

American cowboys borrowed many customs from the Mexican *vaqueros* who had herded cattle in Texas.

Chapter 1

The Cowboy in America

The American cowboy tradition began in Spain. Big groups, or herds, of cattle lived in a dry climate. They needed to search across large areas to find enough grass to eat. Only someone on horseback could keep up with these cattle.

When the Spanish **colonized** Mexico and parts of the American Southwest, they brought their cowboy traditions with them. A Mexican cowboy was called a *vaquero* (ba-KER-o), from the Spanish word *vaca* (BA-ka), or "cow." Women could not be cowboys until later.

English-speaking Americans began to colonize Texas around 1821. They joined their traditions with the Mexican way of cattle ranching. Later, fights in the 1830s and 1840s meant that many Mexicans left Texas. They often left their cattle behind. These herds were later rounded up by new American settlers.

The cattle industry expanded to California and the Rocky Mountains. In these times, there were few fences dividing land. Many cattle owners kept their cows together in one big herd. They hired cowboys to look after the herds and drive, or move, them to market for sale along a route called a trail.

Moving West

Americans moved west for many reasons: to better follow their cultural or religious traditions, to make money, or to escape crowded cities. Land was plentiful and cheap. Many people moved simply for the adventure. Once they settled, they often wrote to friends and family, urging them to follow.

The West was a new, open country that lured many adventurous settlers. Some of them became cowboys.

In the Old West, most boys learned to ride horses at an early age.

Chapter 2

Becoming a Cowboy

In the West, most families had one or two horses. Horse-riding skills were an important part of being a cowboy.

The typical cowboy began as a **wrangler**. Wranglers were in charge of all the other cowboys' horses. Each cowboy usually brought three horses on a long drive. The wrangler made sure the horses were fed, cared for, and ready for action. Though an important job, it did not pay well.

Once a wrangler had more experience, he would graduate to full cowboy. He would ride from sunrise to sunset and learn to rope cattle while on horseback. For all his work, he was paid a dollar a day.

Many Different Cowboys

Even after America claimed Texas in 1845, there were still many cowboys from Mexico living in Texas and elsewhere. After the American Civil War (1861–1865), some former slaves found there was more opportunity in the West. About 15 percent of all cowboys were African American. Native Americans were cowboys, too.

The most important job was trail boss. This very experienced cowboy would be in charge of the entire cattle drive. In the late nineteenth century, he would have earned $90 to $125 every month.

Old cowboys often served as cooks. The cook would ride in a chuck, or food, wagon pulled by oxen. A typical meal would include biscuits, gravy, salt pork, and black coffee.

Bill Pickett

Cowboys were workingmen unlikely to become famous unless they became outlaws or showmen. Bill Picket (1870–1932) was a cowboy of African-American and Cherokee origin who became famous for inventing the technique of "bulldogging." He would leap from his horse and grab male cattle, called steers, by the horns and wrestle them to the ground.

River crossings were one of the most dangerous parts of a cattle drive.

Chapter 3

A Day on the Cattle Drive

Ranchers, not cowboys, owned the cattle. Cowboys were employed by the ranchers. Because big cities or railways were often far from cattle ranches, the cattle had to be moved hundreds of miles for sale or slaughter.

A typical herd would have about three thousand cows. Some fifteen cowboys were needed to drive them. Most drives began in early spring. That way, the rivers wouldn't have flooded yet, making them easy for cattle and horses to cross. Also, the cattle could eat new spring grass.

The cowboy's day began with an early breakfast. Then he helped drive the cattle until lunch at noon.

While the cowboys ate, the cattle grazed. Then they started down the trail again until bedtime.

Cowboys couldn't drive the cattle too fast or they wouldn't have time to eat. They would lose weight and become less valuable. Most herds could travel 10 to 12 miles (16 to 19 kilometers) each day.

A Cowboy's Day

3 a.m.	The cook starts making breakfast
6 a.m.	The cowboys hit the trail
12 p.m.	Stop to eat lunch
2 p.m.	Back on the trail
6 p.m.	Make camp, have dinner
8 p.m.	First watch of the night guard

During the day, cowboys took breaks for meals.

Cowboys worked in different positions in the herd. The best positions were in the front, leading the herd. The worst were in the back, where cowboys had to breathe a lot of dust.

There were many dangers on the trail. A cowboy might fall from his horse, get hurt or trampled by a steer, or get bitten by a snake. Cattle sometimes drowned or suffered deadly falls.

One of the cowboy's biggest fears was a stampede, meaning the entire herd would run in an uncontrollable panic. They would step on anything in their path or even run off a cliff. Anything that scared the cattle could start a stampede. To stop the stampede, a cowboy had to get ahead of the herd and turn it. He would shout or fire his gun to make the lead animals veer. If he could make them run in a circle, they would get tired and eventually stop. At night, some cowboys would sing to their cattle to keep them calm.

Both cattle and cowboys could be hurt or killed in a stampede.

A lasso was used to rope cattle from horseback.

Chapter 4

The Cowboy's Tools

A cowboy's main tool was his horse. It was usually a **mustang**, a descendant of Spanish horses. There were horses used for herding and horses used for roping cattle. A herding horse was small and quick so it could separate one cow from the herd. Roping horses were usually bigger. They used their weight to help the cowboy control a roped steer.

Most cowboys rode mustangs.

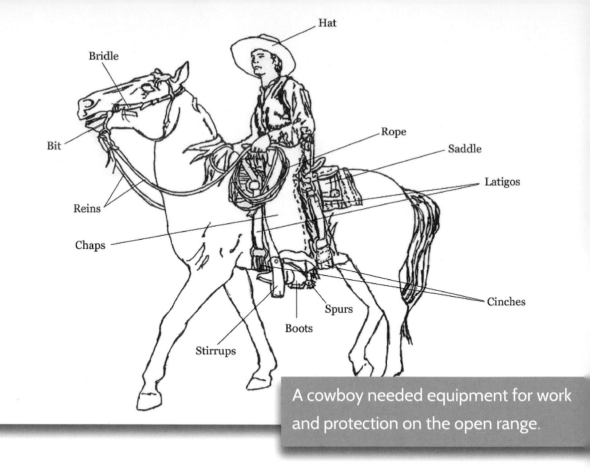

Hat

Bridle

Bit

Reins

Chaps

Rope

Saddle

Latigos

Cinches

Spurs

Boots

Stirrups

A cowboy needed equipment for work and protection on the open range.

The cowboy rode in a Western saddle. It had a high back and front. He could tie his **lasso** onto the front of the saddle when he roped cattle. The bridle and reins were designed to hold in one hand, so the cowboy could lasso with the other.

Each article of a cowboy's clothing served a purpose. The cowboy hat protected him from sun and rain. He could pull his bandanna over his mouth and nose to keep out trail dust. Chaps—leather leggings that buckled over pants—protected the cowboy from thorny bushes as he rode.

Cowboy boots were specially designed for safety. The narrow toe fit easily in the **stirrup**. The heel kept the foot from becoming

Cowboys often wore chaps to protect their legs from brush and thorns.

wedged all the way in the stirrup. That could be deadly if the cowboy was thrown from his horse. The boots were high enough to stay on but loose enough to be easily pulled off if they did get stuck in the stirrup.

Another essential piece of equipment was the lasso. The cowboy would skillfully throw the lasso around cattle's horns or neck to catch them. It might be made of braided rawhide or cotton.

Branding

Before cattle were herded to market, they were rounded up. In the roundup, the cattle would be gathered together so any new calves could be branded, or burned with a heated metal iron. The metal was shaped into letters or designs to show who owned the cattle. The cowboy used his lasso to catch the calf. It would then be held down and branded.

Chapter 5

The Cowboy's Legacy

Barbed wire was invented in the 1860s and came into wide use in the American West in the 1880s. It was a very low-cost item used to fence in huge pieces of land. Ranchers no longer wanted cattle grazing everywhere. They only wanted their cattle on their own land. Cowboys weren't needed for big roundups anymore.

As the West became more populated, towns, trains, and meat-packing

The invention of barbed wire meant the end of the open range.

factories grew closer to ranch land. Long cattle drives were no longer necessary. The cowboy's glory days were over.

Today, most cattle are transported by trucks that drive directly to the ranch. Still, cowboys are needed to herd cattle around the ranch and to help with jobs such as branding.

Cowboys are so popular that some ranches invite tourists to re-creations of old cattle drives. Guests can ride alongside real working cowboys. Rodeos are also popular. There, cowboys can display skills such as riding, roping, and steer wrestling. There are also many women, called cowgirls, involved.

The cowboy helped shape the American West, and his legacy lives on today.

Today, cowboys still work on ranches and display their skills at rodeos.

Glossary

American West The land of the United States west of the Mississippi River.

colonize When a country sends some of its people to live in a new country.

lasso A rope with a loop at one end, used for catching cattle or other animals.

mustang A wild or semi-wild horse in the American West descended from Spanish horses.

rancher A person who owns or manages a cattle farm.

stampede A sudden wild running of a large group of animals.

stirrup The pair of small rings that hold the feet of a rider. Stirrups are attached to a saddle by a strap.

wrangler The cowboy who is in charge of taking care of horses.

Find Out More

Books

Olson, Tod. *How To Get Rich on a Texas Cattle Drive*. Washington, DC: National Geographic, 2010.

Schlissel, Lillian. *Black Frontiers: A History of African American Heroes in the Old West*. New York: Aladdin, 2000.

Staton, Hilarie N. *All About America: Cowboys and the Wild West*. New York: Kingfisher, 2011.

Website

National Cowboy and Western Heritage Museum Website: Diamond R Ranch

cowboykids.nationalcowboymuseum.org

Video

***All About Cowboys for Kids*, Parts 1 and 2**
Directed by Tom McComas and Joseph Stachler. TM Books & Video, 2004. DVD.

Index

Page numbers in **boldface** are illustrations. Entries in **boldface** are glossary terms.

About the Author

Laura L. Sullivan is the author of more than thirty fiction and nonfiction books for children, including the fantasies *Under the Green Hill* and *Guardian of the Green Hill*. She has written many books for Cavendish Square. She would love to have been a cowgirl ... if she wasn't allergic to horses.